Once Again

Once Again

Poems by
Victor di Suvero

Copyright ©2016 by Victor di Suvero. ALL RIGHTS RESERVED.

All rights to poems previously published in magazines, chapbooks and books are retained by the author and all poems which are being published for the first time hereby have all reprint rights assigned to the author. These rights include, but by no means whatsoever are limited to, any means of recording or reproducing the material through oral or visual means including videotape, film, and records.

FIRST EDITION 2016

10 9 8 7 6 5 4 3 2 1

LIBRARY OF CONGRESS CATALOG CARD NUMBER: 2016940226
ISBN: 978-0-938631-58-3 paper

BOOK DESIGN: SunFlower Elliott, SunFlower Designs of Santa Fe
TYPEFACE: Perpetua

Published by
PENNYWHISTLE PRESS, INC.
Victor di Suvero
email: vdisuvero@newmexico.com

Dedication

*This book is dedicated
to my friends, living and dead,
who have shared my voyage through time
in ways that have made this book possible.*

Other books by Victor di Suvero

Salt and the Heart's Horizons
Sight Poems
San Francisco Poems
The Net & Other Poems
Tesuque Poems
naked Heart
Harvest Time
Spring Again
A Gathering
Moving On
Still Here
Considering

Editor:
¡Saludos!
**The Bilingual Anthology
of the Poetry of New Mexico**

Contents

Introduction ~~~~~~~~~~~~~~~~ ix

Once Again ~~~~~~~~~~~~~~~~~ 1

How Did We Come Here? ~~~~~~~~ 2

Yes and Yes ~~~~~~~~~~~~~~~~ 3

Our Work ~~~~~~~~~~~~~~~~~~ 4

And I Could Have Been One Of Them ~~ 5

So Many Years After ~~~~~~~~~~~ 6

An Open Letter ~~~~~~~~~~~~~~ 7

Tomorrow ~~~~~~~~~~~~~~~~~ 10

Time ~~~~~~~~~~~~~~~~~~~~ 11

Best To Be Ready ~~~~~~~~~~~~ 12

To Begin Again ~~~~~~~~~~~~~ 13

Empty Words ~~~~~~~~~~~~~~ 15

Chance ~~~~~~~~~~~~~~~~~~ 16

It Is Truly Wonderful ~~~~~~~~~~ 17

Time Is All We Have ~~~~~~~~~~ 18

Time Teaches ~~~~~~~~~~~~~~ 19

For Love That's Given ~~~~~~~~~~ 20

Look Forward Not Back ~~~~~~~~ 21

Poem On Demand for My Neighbor Jose 22

For Barbara *September 14th 2015* ~~~ 23

As Requested ~~~~~~~~~~~~~~ 24

The Family Story ~~~~~~~~~~~~ 25

To Henrietta ~~~~~~~~~~~~~~~ 26

How Many ~~~~~~~~~~~~~~~~ 27

Poem For The First Of May ~~~~~~ 28

Truth ~~~~~~~~~~~~~~~~~~~ 29

When One Falls ~~~~~~~~~~~~~ 30

It's A New Way ~~~~~~~~~~~~~ 31

About Time ~~~~~~~~~~~~~~~ 32

All Of Them ~~~~~~~~~~~~~~~ 33

On Our Butts ~~~~~~~~~~~~~~ 34

We Are Here ~~~~~~~~~~~~~~ 35

Timing ~~~~~~~~~~~~~~~~~~ 36

A Luxury ~~~~~~~~~~~~~~~~ 37

Winter Solstice III ~~~~~~~~~~~ 38

Wondering ~~~~~~~~~~~~~~~ 39

To Live With The Beloved ~~~~~~~ 40

For Alexander ~~~~~~~~~~~~~~ 41

To My Daughter Romana ~~~~~~~ 42

Contents

For Gavilan ~~~~~~~~~~~~~~~~~ 43

The Practice Of Sacrifice ~~~~~~~~~ 44

Even In Winter ~~~~~~~~~~~~~~ 45

Timor Mortis ~~~~~~~~~~~~~~~ 46

When One Is Chosen ~~~~~~~~~~ 47

Duende ~~~~~~~~~~~~~~~~~~~ 48

Repetition ~~~~~~~~~~~~~~~~~ 49

Question ~~~~~~~~~~~~~~~~~~ 50

Lonely ~~~~~~~~~~~~~~~~~~~~ 51

Earnings ~~~~~~~~~~~~~~~~~~ 52

A Comfort Zone ~~~~~~~~~~~~~ 53

For Papa ~~~~~~~~~~~~~~~~~~ 54

For Mami ~~~~~~~~~~~~~~~~~~ 55

This One Is For Yanko Varda ~~~~~~ 56

Money ~~~~~~~~~~~~~~~~~~~~ 57

The Illusion Of Control ~~~~~~~~~ 58

Not Good Enough ~~~~~~~~~~~~ 59

Easter Morning ~~~~~~~~~~~~~~ 60

Sea Song ~~~~~~~~~~~~~~~~~~ 61

The Adriatic ~~~~~~~~~~~~~~~~ 63

A Chance Meeting ~~~~~~~~~~~ 64

For All Of Us ~~~~~~~~~~~~~~~ 65

The Two Cousins ~~~~~~~~~~~~ 66

Riff #10 ~~~~~~~~~~~~~~~~~~~ 67

At La Villita ~~~~~~~~~~~~~~~~ 70

Autumn Leaves ~~~~~~~~~~~~~~ 72

Are They The Same? ~~~~~~~~~~ 74

The Same Thing ~~~~~~~~~~~~~ 75

What Is Your Name? ~~~~~~~~~~ 76

¿Cuál es Tu Nombre? ~~~~~~~~~~ 77

We Do Not Own ~~~~~~~~~~~~ 78

No Somos Los Dueños ~~~~~~~~~ 79

Rediscovering Books On A Shelf ~~~~~ 80

An Empire's End ~~~~~~~~~~~~ 81

Poem For Beni Israel ~~~~~~~~~~ 82

Another Way Of Looking At It ~~~~~~ 82

We Are Fortunate ~~~~~~~~~~~~ 83

Honoring All Veterans ~~~~~~~~~ 84

Curious ~~~~~~~~~~~~~~~~~~~ 85

About The Author ~~~~~~~~~~~ 87

Introduction
by Bruce Moss

When you read the poems of Victor di Suvero in this volume you will realize you are in the presence of a poet whose thoughts and feelings, transmuted into lines of verse, will move you as if those thoughts and feelings were your own. He is not a poet who retreats into obscurity, challenging you to guess his meaning and intent. His lines speak directly to your own experience of life, so that you think, "Ah, you too!" His poetry will provoke you into lightning glimpses into your own cache of emotional memory that might have lain buried by the detritus of life in our 21st Century.

Victor is a poet whose range is wide and deep. You will find lines written by a man who has sharply experienced life and who does not hold back from suggesting how to live it. In *Time is All We Have,* he writes, "...the only one / Argument for the good life is economy / Achieved by not wasting time on guilts, / Regrets or even penances." In *We Are Here,* he counsels, "We wake at dawn, pleased we have been given / Another day to work, to play, to read, to shout / Or dance, sing and even pray since tomorrow is / Still not promised to any one of us." Memento mori are stinging arrows in any poet's quiver, but Victor's focus is on the joyful days the present offers us, if we'll take them.

And always, the poetry sings, words and phrases striking chords that remind us that our spirit can yet again be moved, whatever our age or situation. His thoughts on love and relationship are caught for display in *To Live with the Beloved,* with "To live with the beloved / One must learn to be up / With the dawn for its blessings / To wash dishes as sacrament / To clean the house in ways / That are luminous.../ Otherwise the days are numbered, the sand / Is measured out, the fabric tears, expressions / Ring hollow, the bud withers / And one is no longer there / At all." The theme of carrying water and chopping wood in the service of love has rarely been so elegantly proposed.

Reading Victor's poems is like wandering through a rich garden filled with exotic flowers and fruits, yet all the while gently teaching us lessons he himself has learned on his own life's journey. To an acquisitive world he raises a finger with *We Do Not Own,* cautioning, "You don't own the four directions, child, / They own you. The mountain owns you. / The meadows by the river ... / This is the place in which to rest, / The place to be, knowing you will not / Ever own it if you count on staying free."

With *When One is Chosen* he flips the equation on love, knowing as the ancients did that it is a magical property of the deities, that we can no more will ourselves to fall in love than we can will ourselves to be reborn—"Having been reminded once again / That it is Love that chooses one and / That no matter how one tries / No one, no person can choose Love, / Ever, in any way at all."

His poem *To Henrietta* is Victor at his intensely moving best. He has had the sudden urge to phone his ex-wife, the most natural thing in the world when something occurs that we want to share with someone once so close. The poem opens with "It's so silly." Such a light-hearted word, silly. And it is light-hearted for a reason. When he remembers, slapping his head, that she died four years ago, he is relieved: she is actually not dead at all. She is present, her spirit is with him. The classically religious idea that after we die our soul goes to heaven, hell or purgatory, "Had been put together to discipline / The daily activities of the living / And really had nothing to do with / The dead other than a discipline." So though his heart yearns at the moment for the once-wife, and the summer's days they shared, all is well in the universe: Henrietta is close by. So silly. So poignant.

In *Autumn Leaves* the poet sings of summer's end, "Stillness / In the air. The world is waiting / And all that has to be done / Is being done one day at a time."

And from the vantage point of his eighth decade, he gives us relief in *A Chance Meeting*. "I have just met the Angel of Death / She is sweet and charming / And not at all as scary / As we have all been / Brought up to think…"

In Victor's work there are births and rebirths, shocks of recognition, startled rediscoveries of delights long forgotten, sweet in their freshness. Few are sweeter than *Rediscovering Books on a Shelf*: "I find myself reading Poetry these days as if I had already died / And returned for an hour or so to get back to those shelves / Where I had filed so many of those books that had taught me / To think, to see, to sing and to cry as well as to pray / From time to time…"

"We all were born," he writes in At *La Villita*, "in that sea which filled / Our mothers' wombs before we came out / To breathe air as we have learned to do…"

And when we are gone, he cautions in *Empty Words*, "It is not bone and muscle that remain, / Not tongue, not brain, but words alone / That sing and come back again with / Tears and joy and pride and tenderness / To shine and shape our days."

Victor's cantabile lines bring us glad tidings in our present world of mistrust, crass salesmanship, and abandoned belief systems. Love, wonder and rebirth can be found, he tells us, if we look. He is profoundly suited to such visions, this Venetian-born man who grew up in China, who sailed the sea in the American Merchant Marine, lived for years in California, and dwells now in the High Desert of New Mexico.

Bruce Moss *is the Santa Fe writer of the novels* The Outside Man, Under Black Stars, *and* Desert Electra.

Once Again

Once again we begin
With the morning sun's rays
Chasing the dark of night
Out of the sky
            And we face
Another day of challenges
From making up the bed
So that it will be ready
Tonight and then getting up
To feed the body
For today.
            Yes, once again
To reach into the drawer
Where I store my stash of hope
To take out this day's portion
So that I will have enough
With me to keep me going
All day and into the evening
Because without it we all
Have a tendency to find a bench
In the park or in front of the church
And stay there all day
Doing nothing at all.

So we always do need our daily
Piece of hope. So as to smile
And say hello to all our friends.

How Did We Come Here?

What was it that drew us here?
Was it the land calling, the piñon?
The great shaped clouds blessing the
Blue of the sky? Was it the dawn's quiet or the
Other one, the one that comes after the day of
Work, at dusk in summer, promising rest and
Respite and all the other good things we dream of
When we let ourselves do so?

How did we come here? Was it the wind? Or was
It the star that moved us, all of us?

Tell me about the Anasazi, how they came here,
Out of the Earth's navel, the Sipapu, the hole in
The ground made by Coyote when Lightning came
After him — tell me about the old ones, the ones
Who came from over the edge by starlight, riding
The wind, driven by hope as well as by terror —
Tell me!

How is it that we came here, to cottonwoods?
We brought our cooking pots
And histories and prayers, we brought our
Hopes to make a place where the children's
Children not yet born may come to tell each other
Stories of how it is that we came here and why —
And they may end up knowing more about it than
We do now.

I have come to give thanks to wind
And star and call of land,
All those that served to bring us here.

Yes and Yes

We can believe in all the negatives
That the world throws continually
In our way but then we must return
To all the positives and say yes
And yes so that we may find
Reasons to continue to be alive
Knowing so many of the reasons
That made so many kill and be killed.

Look at all the monuments
The statues and the paintings
Celebrating the achievements
Of this one who conquered a country
And that one who saved another.
Always negating what was
In your hand as you said the rosary
Because you were taught to believe,
And yes the miracles did happen
And all the ways that the ones
Who wanted to believe made it up
And over the stairs all the way to the
Top where one could see so far
Beyond horizons all the way to the stars
Which is why the Jews invented
Hollywood and the telescopes
On Mauna Kea to bring the stars
Home to roost.

Our Work

We deal in surprises. Our magic
Turns words into delights or tears.
We remind, recall and represent.
With us, complaints become eloquence
And when anger is vented by us even
Revolutions can be fired up by
What we do.   Lonely and alone even
While dancing or whipping up a crowd
We give people reasons to fall in love,
To rediscover the universe, and to
Learn about hope in winter — yes, and
To believe even in themselves.

Our own experience becomes a
Mirror for all those who read
And hear our work.   Older than
Iron mongers we are those whose
Craft was learned in caves even
Before the great temples were
Raised to honor Ishtar and Isis.

We praise Orion and sing for
The Seven Sisters remembering
To see even when blinded and
To hear even when we are deaf
So as to be voice and vanguard
For all that happens here.

And I Could Have Been One Of Them

The snow fell all night last night. This
Morning, walking through it, the half mile
Down the hill to get the Sunday paper and
Back up as the cold mist turned the world
Into black and white like those old photos
Of the war in Russia, I understood in a new way
How it must have been for the boys in that
Division of the Italian Army green at
16 and 17, sent up to the Russian Front
By Mussolini, at Hitler's demand.
Stalingrad.

Out of the sunbaked hill towns, the groves
Where lemons, oranges and olives came from,
The untrained fodder for the Russian guns
Went, ill-clothed, with gloves so thin
The fingers froze. The sixty thousand men
And officers of the Blue Division turned blue
And died — all but eleven hundred and sixty-two,
Who somehow managed to make it through
And get back to Italy.

Fifty-four years have gone by and it's all
One now, even the memory. Fifty-eight
Thousand and some may not be so many, but
The stupidity of even one event like that in
The light of the millions dead freezes the heart.

How will I be able to tell my children how stupid
This generation of ours has been and how
Stupidly this waste keeps on wasting us all away,
In Afghanistan, in Israel, in Florida and in the town
Next door as it did in 'Nam and now Rwanda,
Sierra Leone, Timor and the high desert
Where we now live.

So Many Years After

Watching an old movie the other night
As we have come to do to be together
The story of the "Lion of the Desert"
Presented itself in ways that spoke
To me not only in terms of the history
It portrayed, the fight of the Bedouins
Against the Italian occupation and
The employment by the Fascist occupiers
Of everything from poison gas to tanks,
Machine guns and artillery to subdue them.
To sit there and see how
Those Bedouins whose land had been taken and
Those who rode their horses and had only rifles
In the 9th year of the Fascist era and to
Realize again that my own grandfather,
The Admiral Millo, was the one who had
Accepted the surrender of the Bey of Tripoli
When in 1911 he had become the hero
Who had retaken the old shore, Libya,
From which the Trojans had come
To become Romans and the forerunners of
All those Fascists that came after.
It was strange to see enacted so much
Of what I had lived through as a boy,
Black shirt, the Fascist Salute evolved
By Mussolini from the ancient Roman greeting,
The correctness of the uniforms, the medals,
The specificity of the orders, the sense
That in the beginning of the 20th Century
It was the Italians who had built the first,
The very first concentration camps and set
The pattern for Dachau, for Korea, Vietnam
And now for Afghanistan and that I am here
Still alive, aware that it was that branch
Of our family tree that had initiated all
That we were so fortunate to have escaped.

An Open Letter in the form of a Poem addressed to the Honorable Trustees of the United States Holocaust Memorial Museum.

Magnificently and awesomely arranged, beginning with the beginning
Of the Nazi Assault. Once again beginning the elimination of the Jews
From the face of the earth, a repetition of the original elimination
Attempt much grander in scale than the wipe out in York in England
In 1185 — remember the Last of the Just? — and in so many other
Places and times — Why are we here?
                                                            But this grey Mausoleum is
Technically correct from the facts of Kristallnacht to the shutting
Of the shops, to the beginnings of the roundups, the conversion
Of hospitals into the first slaughter houses.
                                                     And all so perfectly
Displayed when I suddenly felt the rush of air conditioned air,
The clean air moving around the visitors and realized then
That the Stench was missing — that was it — the smells, the shit,
The stink that only comes from dead bodies in the ditches all
Full of excrement of all kinds, guts spilling out, skulls split open
And all the rot that could be seen.... but the Smell
Was Not There — like taking someone who is blind
To a show of Rodin's — and even in the one boxcar standing there,
Exemplar of the thousands that had carried the thousand
Thousands to the Killing Centers, clean, swept out, without
The smell of fear, of vomit, of the torn lives, the piss, the sweat
Not a whiff,
                Then further, as if in a power point presentation gone
Wrong, mumbled memories of survivors, boxed in a glass cage....
But where was the sound of rifle butts on an old woman's back,
Where the sniffles, the muffled desperation, the cries of children
Sucking on dried breasts? No sound except the murmur
Of the viewers.

Then the shoes, we've all heard about them,
The piles of them, silent, stenchless, as if fumigated and
Dusted with the talc of time with no hint of the smell
Of the feet that had inhabited them. Feet yes, suddenly making
Me think of the feet of Christ, that other Jew, nailed to the Cross

In the thousands of Crucifixes above altars in churches that show
The blood and the nails and the Crown of Thorns but so clearly
That they have become Art and have little to do with Calvary anymore
That other Killing Field. Before Christianity, before the Crusades.
And then to turn and
Suddenly
Confront the smoke belching out of the two towering chimneys
At Buchenwald and out of the other rendering plants with no, nein, kein,
Absolutely no smell at all, no sense of all the roasting that had
Gone on and on....

Duties, every single thing legal, ordnung, papers
To show authority, the final solution, but where's the Smell?
Where's the stink of it?....and the sounds, the beatings,
The bones breaking, those last cries?....but no, we are shown
Early models of IBM machines used to file the tattooed numbers
And then leaving
   Because it had become too much to swallow, chilled,
Realizing that but for fate and circumstance my face
Could have been that one....on the 13 year old staring at me
Out of the picture of the ones in one of the boxcars, wondering,
Where he was going, all in his face
But my parents had been fortunate and we had made it here
To San Francisco that February in 1941 never to forget
How close the call....yes we need reminding....
And need the Smells to truly know what it was like.

Then, after a couple of years of learning about life,
Here in the US so far from everything else,
Lucky, I shipped out as a Merchant Seaman in the Pacific
During the War and sailed down to Guadalcanal, the Russell Islands,
Lae, Hollandia, Biak, and the landings at Leyte and Lingayen Gulf
Where I learned about the smell of death
With my own nose but
That smell was clean by comparison and for the sake of the truth of what
                                        did happen ➤➤

And for all the times to come so that the memories will live,
Go get a shit machine, blow that smell through the galleries, build
A sound track of the beatings, the gurgling in the gas chambers
And do let those smells and sounds
Float through the galleries even
Though it may end up reducing attendance
So the story can stay alive in more than words and pictures.

Yes, you may even decide to bottle it and sell the Smell
At the counter along with the incense sticks labeled
Dachau or Marisenstadt so that visitors could leave
With a piece of the Holocaust to take home and smell it
From time to time and to let their children also
To know that that smell is one still to be remembered

Sincerely yours.
Victor di Suvero
Alcalde, NM 2009

Tomorrow

For how many of us does one more day
Count as a blessing or a tribulation?
One more day with hope
Or one more day with pain?

Questions for which there never are
Answers of any kind.

We all reach a point in time
When that one more day
Becomes more important
Than any other we can remember.

And it comes as surely
As the sun sets
And the night comes on
To count the ways
In which we are
With ourselves and
With all the others
In our lives.

Just one more day.

Time

Time was an early invention
Of our human kind structuring
Hours, minutes and seconds to
Measure out the waiting for
A lover's return or the start
Of work or even getting on a train.
Our universe had given us days
And months, seasons and even years
To count, but time itself and our
Perception of it, fast or slow,
Depending on each situation was
And is what we deal with
In our daily lives.   So much of it
Already past and no way of
Knowing how much is left for
Each and everyone of us and yet
We keep it when we can, spending
As much as we may care to
In pursuit of money, love, care,
Comfort, security, fame and all
The other things that make up
Our timeless lives.

Best To Be Ready

The family icon is a 12th Century Pilgrim shell
With a carving of the "Flight into Egypt" — Joseph
And Mary with the child Jesus on the donkey,
A cherub overhead gentle in its message
Of going for safety, for life, and to this day
There does not seem to be a record of their return.

No stories in the Gospels or the Apocrypha of how
It was they made it back to Nazareth, even
To Jerusalem or even about those years lost
Between the throwing of the money changers out
Of the Temple to the Garden of Gethsemane
Which led to Calvary and the Resurrection.
                                                              No
Mention of those years of growing up and going on,
Perhaps to India, some say, inspiring pilgrimages
And other travels around the world.
                                        When asked
Why a Sephardic family would have such a shell
To pass on over the generations my Father said
"It's all right, you see, Son, when they went off to Egypt
"There were no Catholics, no Christians, no Protestants.
"They had other things to fight about or to pray to,
"Or for."
             "It's just a reminder to keep on going
"So long as you can and then be sure to tell
"Your children and theirs it's always best to be ready
"To be on the go, moving on," he said.

To Begin Again

As sun breaks, as gull cries
As fields are tilled
To begin again

As the loved one dies
As hawks wheel
To begin again

As the house burns
And the flood washes away everything
As the friend miscalculates
As bowls break
To begin again

As the direction is lost
And the food runs out
As the orchard is blighted and anger explodes
To begin again

To begin
Each time
Again

From seed to flowering
Without hope of turning
Without prayer
Without hope, without dream

To begin a long journey without water
Having come a long way across deserts
Having eaten camels

To begin again
Knowing the masquerade is complete
Knowing the sum is false
Knowing your partner betrayed you
Yesterday

To begin again
Each time at dawn
As the wind begins to move
And the fleshing of your bones comes true

Each time
Again

The daffodil grows
The river runs
And you turn

To begin
Again

Empty Words

And they say we use empty words
They say "Your words are empty,
They do not hold a thing. It's only
Living flesh that counts — the unique person
Standing there in front of you." And yet

All of us are interchangeable,
Queen Isabella's skull and Montezuma's
Look mightily the same today
And all the world's magnificence
Fades into gray as we go on.

It is not bone and muscle that remain,
Not tongue, not brain, but words alone
That sing and come back again with
Tears and joy and pride and tenderness
To shine and shape our days.

We are blessed with voices; let us then
Praise it all, even the pain, the bad choices
And the falling rain; praising fish
And birds and children out at play
Knowing that our empty words are still
The only keepers of our dreams and histories.

Chance

Chance, Fate, the Luck of the Draw,
Karma in all its manifestations —
The seasons of the heart that have
No reason, all are integral in our lives,
No matter how we plan them or have
Them planned for us.
              We learn to work
And talk and eventually to play our roles,
Learning to be pleasant and to get along
Learning to learn so as to become true,
Brave, strong and even learn to play
While engaging ourselves by doing good
For others in their needs not even
Thinking that we ourselves become
At times Luck itself for others while
Also learning to be with each other without
Jealousy, greed, anger or even hate.
              We, yes,
We are the ones who, having made this world
Our home and place know that gentleness
And grace are possible and that we can
Still overcome the politicians and the grifters
That we have allowed to screw the beauty
Of this world of ours into a killing field.

Who knows why? Is it because of Chance
Or Fate, or of that Luck I spoke about or even of
That Karma in all the ways it works?
Please let me know when you
Find out.

It Is Truly Wonderful

It is truly wonderful how we go on
Without thinking
Until death, divorce, or war,
One of the great severance,
Comes along and demands that the ledgers
Be audited, examined,
So as to see that the various entries
Tally with the end result which brought
The self to its present pass.

Some of us stop there,
At the pass, and,
Cozened by the very newness of thought
Find ourselves buried in an avalanche
Of snowy reflections,
Or frozen by the the wind of recriminations;

And we forget that beyond the pass
There lie the rich countries
Burgeoning green in the watered valleys,
Which can only be reached
By bringing heart and motion to bear.

Time Is All We Have

Time is all we have, to give, to use,
To share with the beloved, time is all
We have — given to us as long
As body's strength permits us life —
All else does not belong to us —
Stewards of one kind or another,
Caretakers or wastrels, good ones,
Bad ones and some in between,
Solitary, gregarious, committed
To a cause or to acquisitions
We share this passage we call time
While doing all the other things we do.

We sleep, sing, dance and work, bring
Children into the world while killing
Enemies as well as animals and birds.
With each and every act of ours we take
Pieces of our capital without remorse.
Every single thing takes time — sleep
Takes time, stupidity as well — the only one
Argument for the good life is economy
Achieved by not wasting time on guilts,
Regrets or even penances.　　　　Time's faces,
The dark one and the light, are the faces
Of our lives — sad and somber,
Serious and wondrous, bright and full
Of laughter from one moment to another
When we notice them reflected
In the mirrors of our time
As we move along our voyages
In the concourse of the stars.

Time Teaches

Time teaches us to serve the arts
As acolytes are trained. Some of us
Simply remain there, in training,
Raising money, sending newsletters out
Into the world, forgetting to graduate,
Forgetting the one point of it,
The joy of being and of
This world we can enjoy with smiles.

It's all here in this high desert:
A daughter's wedding coming in the Fall,
The sound of hooves drumming on the wind,
The wry smile of a friend dead too soon of AIDS,
The working dreams of a new house,
While politicians play their shabby games;
The winds of friendship are serene and good and
Even Othello Simpson's looming presence on CNN
Does not undo our sense of right
As the Spring's first crocus springs into the hands of lovers
And children run to play —
                        Learning
A piece of music can teach us how to hear
The cantata of the streets, the odes of clouds
And the songs immanent in the voice
Of the beloved.
                    In the film, "The Madness
"Of King George," it is Cordelia's speech
To her Dad, sweet, impossible and mad
Old Lear; and then her kiss upon his cheek
That heals the King.
                       Poetry does serve all
Of us — even as the seasons and the horses do —
As lovers serve each other in the night of days
And in the day of nights while time
Teaches us to serve as we go along our ways.

For Love That's Given

When payment of any kind
Is expected by the giver
It's not love that's given —

Seed planted in receiving earth
Gives all to stalk of wheat,
Apple tree or fir
Without regret —
It gives and giving all
Fulfills its role.

Ask no return
Of child, lover
Or even the busy world.

It comes
When it's not asked, as wind comes,
Or rain — unexpectedly —

And then
Comes back again
Again.

Look Forward Not Back

Look forward not back
It's tough but easier on the eyes
Don't cry for what went wrong
Laugh for what's going right
No prayers for the impossible
Just thanks for the best thing done
Big sails to catch the wind
Strong rudder to get there.

All the pebbles on the shore
Have histories of their own,
Each one.
          Tall trees smile
With the sun every time
The sun comes out.
              My
Own life has had so many
Facets I cannot understand
It any more.
          The ones you meet
May change the way you look
At the world as well as the
Way the world looks at you
You cannot wake to all the possibilities
Unless you have been asleep for a while.
Never forgetting the difficulties
And how you dealt with them.

Lay me down to sleep now
So I may awake ready
Once more to take it
All on.
My prayer as I have not
Prayed in a long time.

Poem On Demand For My Neighbor Jose —

There are those of us who find delight
And celebrate the fact that they have
Finally found their beloved and
Celebrate the thought that they actually
Might look forward to a year with
The beloved as the achievement of all
Their prior prayers and hopes.
                                        And then
The year comes and turns into two
Before the lovers realize it because
Their love is true and each day
Becomes another discovery and
Pleasure continues to destroy
The concept of ordinary time so
That the days and months and
Years flow into each other so that
Before either one can really count
Time appears to disappear.
                                     And
Suddenly when the lovers are made
To count by the arrival of one child
And then two and more so that
The continued pleasure becomes
That which is basic in their lives
And then they stop one day, amazed
And say in full surprise "My Lord
"It's been fifty years already" and
the other one says "you still can't
"Count, my darling last week was
"The beginning of the sixtieth year!"

At which point they both fell back,
Laughing, saying "You still
"Cannot count" to each other
As they began to smile at
The beginning of their 61st year
Together.

For Barbara *September 14th 2015*

This time, when you are away
I came to understand again
That every single thing in my life
To date has helped me to
Get here, to know how much
Of my life has shaped my loving you.
My time in school in China,
My working on the ships during the war,
My digging for the sapphires in Montana,
My writing all I have done to date,
All has been done to make me
The one that can love you
In so many ways as you never
Have been loved before because
You are the shining one
The one whose life sings
Even when you are silent
The one who makes the world
Happen as you choose
Generous and open hearted
So I sing you a true wish
That you may have a truly
HAPPY BIRTHDAY
And a continuing happy time
In all the ways you want
From here on out with joy
And smiles in all the ways
You might want to have!

As Requested

It was new
And yet the feeling
That had entered
His heart evoked
Past histories

He had read
Of great loves

That had caused
Great poets to write
Great works such as
The Divine Comedy
Or the Odyssey

All of which served
To make him realize

His feelings now
Were cut out of
The same cloth
That had served
Dante and Homer.

Not Beatrice and
Not Helen of Troy.

This one had her own
Beauty and ability
To captivate anyone
She chose to fix
In her sights

Or in her own heart
And she, knowing it,

Did not use her power
Casually, she instead
Was very careful
As to where she chose
To exert her powers.

The Family Story

Minor priests, associated in the Temple, money lenders,
Bankers, naval officers, traders, architects and poets, nurses,
Builders, cartographer, musicians, and ladies of all kinds,
Brave ones, beautiful, devoted and brainy ones.
A strange lot, buffeted by winds that carried omens,
Somehow always managing to find a donkey, as in the
Past, to get away, or tickets on a ship or plane these days
To carry us from there to here, from danger to a place
Of safety or even temporary rest.
                                   We've always looked
To be on the move, accommodating to the customs of
The place, adapting each time to the strictures that
Made it possible for one generation of our own
To turn into the next.
                        Always this apparent need to
Make a mark, leave an imprint on the sand, build
Bridges, shape water and make a solid out of time.
We are for a moment only, breathing one breath at a time,
Persisting, no matter what it is we do, learning
Each day how to live forever while concurrently
Learning how to die tomorrow at the same time.

To Henrietta

It's so silly!
Here I was walking around the house
A few minutes ago when I could not
Wait to get to the phone to call you
When I hit my head with my left palm
Remembering you had died in October
Four years ago and that I did not
Need to use the phone to get you.
                                        So,
I am talking to your spirit, or call it
What you will, to let you know
There are times you are quite present
As you were when I discussed mortality
And life thereafter with two friends
Yesterday. Each one of the three of us
With a different idea of what happens
When we die.
                    We did, however, all agree
That the classical idea of the soul going
To heaven or to purgatory or even hell
Had been put together to discipline
The daily activities of the living
And really had nothing to do with
The dead other than a discipline.

Strange really how cathedrals have
Been built among other monuments
To celebrate that which does not exist
Which is a long way round to say
I miss you, lady, but you are
Still around and I hope and trust
You are enjoying this lovely summer day
In whatever form your essence has taken
For itself so be well and love to you
This lovely summer's day.

How Many

How many Easters do we have to celebrate?
Their calendar, our calendar, our version
Their — belief systems of all kinds —
The Last Supper....and was Mary
Of Magdala really there? On this night?
And the version painted by Titian
That ended up to be known as
"The feast in the house of Levi" in Venice
Was it our house then? The house
Of our ancestors?....and then the Gospels.

History has it there were more than four
But the Bishops at Nicea settled on Mark
And James and John and Luke and the others
Were not acknowledged....all in the name
Of orthodoxy ...at least in that church
....and if all the known Gods
As well as those unknown by us were
To party in heaven, with Vishnu and
Buddha and those that would have come
From the Amazon, from Macchu Picchu and
The others from Australia and Tasmania
And the Emperor Gods from Japan — I can hear
Them laughing and enjoying all the sacrifices
Made in all that time before to Jove
And to Juno and Athena and Vespa
With the incense swirling and the laughter
As well as all the sacrifices made to them.

Discipline
Now and for as long a we need
To believe.

Poem For The First Of May

Mayday in certain parts of this world
Is the day to celebrate the work of workers
Because it really is the return of Spring
That will make worker's work a bit better
It's also because of bad translation
      from the French
M'aidez or "help me" got to be known
      as "mayday" in English
Which is the signal for help internationally
So when we use it it can stand
      for what we choose
I choose it to be the day that opens hearts
And helps me to be as delighted
      as possible
In this current life of mine.

Truth

Truth is lovely and She's fair
She has to be presented quietly, exhibited,
Discussed and shown in the best light;
At times She even has to be explained
As the result of a long chain of events,
Viewed, reviewed and even interpreted,
Clearly, before She can be accepted.

Politically, She always engenders difficulties,
Particularly when one group of people want
Something that another group has or wants
Or does not want, or even hates, or loves
As in candidates, representatives or even flags.

In Love She can be either the sweetest
Or the most impossible to bear, even
When spoken to, or about, children, parents,
Let alone the Beloved.
                        We also know that
In Commerce She generally manages to seem
Something altogether different and
Is hardly ever invoked publicly for fear
That if She were to speak She would most
Probably succeed in ruining the transaction.

And then, when Religion comes into Play
She is invoked in so many different
Manifestations that She has a tendency
To disappear altogether since the Management
Of Illusions has never made Her comfortable.

And yet we all claim we want Her, Her Beauty,
Her Firmness and we do want Her always
To be all our own.

When One Falls

When one falls
Down from a ledge in Yosemite
Or out of the back of a truck
One falls and gets hurt
No matter what the specific
Circumstances might be
And one ends up in the hospital
Or even in dire circumstances
At home — and hopefully
One survives.
              And yet
There is another kind of fall
As when one "falls in Love"
For which there is no way
To then deal with hospitals
Or other medical responses,

One just falls and pays
The price.

It's A New Way

The fields are sere and withered with
Winter's grip so plainly there the tree
Is but a skeleton of itself
And yet we're in an age when
Vistas of summer songs and meadows
Full of flowers provide our eyes
With festivals of color given the invention
Of the laptop and its window into
All those other worlds, summers past
And springs of long ago.
                               It's not as
It used to be when we only had
Memory to draw upon, now we
Do not have to remember things as
We had to then — we can just proceed
To manage the thousands of things recorded
In the memory banks of this machine.

A crutch perhaps or rather more like
The invention of the telescope that brought
Distances right up to us and made
Us see that with its help we got to see stars and
So many things as this
Laptop does for us today.

About Time

When I count the hours still left to me
To sit or wonder
Around this home and garden
Or to explore the canyons of my various histories
I am amazed how they spill out
Like marbles out of a sack and become
Absolutely uncountable as they tumble down
Into this sunset at the end of May.
                                      I stoop
As I attempt to pick them up and almost
Fall, but straightening up I find I can
Still throw my shoulders back and stride
Into the evening not thinking about counting
Or any other specific thing but just aware,
Aware of being still alive and walking
Even into a future that will not be measured
By anyone except by itself when it chooses
To do so and not before.

All Of Them

This one in the print
That one in the red
The other one in a dress
That made every man
Say "yes."
                A birthday party
For that old geezer
Who's lived a life and a half
And kept his hand in
Where it's always been
Needed most.
                    Surrounded
By well wishers and his very
Special one he lit up the day
As few have ever done.

We were all there
Not just to wish him well
But to acknowledge him
And his voyages that led
Him down to Hell and back
This friendly dude who now
Is hitting his stride again
And all of us were there
To cheer him and his life
Again.

On Our Butts

Yes, some of us have been sailors, sailing
The blue Pacific, the Red Sea and even
The Gulf of Mexico then down the coast
To Patagonia around the bulge of Brazil
But for generations most of us have sat
On chairs at desks, writing, counting,
Working with words and numbers and
Not out in the fields where backs and legs
Grow strong and stronger as children
Come to do the same.
                        No wonder then
That as we age we grow weaker in the calf
Less capable of moving out into the road
To run with all the others whose lives
Have over time moved one foot after the other
Along the furrows in the fields, the hedgerows,
The roads of pilgrimages and even city streets.

And we continue in this new position
When we sit while driving cars or
Being flown about in aeroplanes and
When we go to entertainments such as
The Opera, the Cinema and even the Ballet
Which celebrates the vitality of movement
As much as football or basketball or other
Games that require one to sit in order to enjoy.

So we sit, as we have for all these years, involving
Magic and the stars from this strange position
That has no place in the evolution of our species
From the days we came out of trees to run
Across the plains and hunt, and after that
To work the land so that it would feed us
Quietly until the urges to believe one thing
Or another led us into confrontations that
Have since turned into wars while we continue
To sit and think and wonder as the world goes on.

We Are Here

Yes, we are here, having come from so many
Different places, from across town or across oceans
Traveling our different roads to be together, here.

Our parents and their parents too all had to stretch
To bring us from those elsewheres to this one place
Filled with dreams, hopes and laughters or even
Pain and troubles, but made it all happen so
That we are here together now.
                                        Even the child,
Newborn, was in its mother's womb before it drew
Its first breath, coming here from another place.

Even those of us who came here because of wars,
Fought as always for land, for oil or even peace
Known that we are all joined in this one great
Adventure we call being alive.

We wake at dawn, pleased we have been given
Another day to work, to play, to read, to shout
Or dance, sing and even pray since tomorrow is
Still not promised to any one of us.

It should speak well for all of us if violence could
Be diminished and the ways of being together
With each other are enhanced.
                                        Yes, do turn now
And turn again to each other with a smile or hug
To share this blessing that we are in fact alive
And well and here together
No matter where we came from or when.

Timing

"It's not time, yet." She said, indicating that a
Certain time would come when every single thing
Would be perfect and appropriate and birds
Wearing their best plumage would break into
Song and all the fruit trees in the garden
Would send perfumes and promises of sweetness
Into the air.

        "It's not time, yet!" She said again as
Eve must have said before the apple ripened, as Peter
Must have thought before the cock crowed thrice, as even
Cleopatra is said to have said to her handmaiden when
She brought the basket with the asp inside.

                It is the
Balancing of time that is the greatest art. The fencer
Has to know the exact instant when the avenue
To his opponent's heart is open so as to be able to thrust
And win. The singer has to learn to hold that one
Note for ever and learn not to let it go before its time
To make it right. Even the bartender about to shut
His shop, no matter how anxious he might be to be
On his way home, when asked, if it's not right, will say
"No, it's not time, yet, but it will be soon," and on that
Perception we all rely having learned that timing is
As important as time itself and more than any other
Single thing for when it's wrong cars collide, hearts
Break, futures are lost, children die and worlds
Fall in upon themselves.

A Luxury

Oh, the luxury of belief
That drives some of us into the way
Of good works, charity and sacrifices
And others into taking up the sword
In the name of God against Infidels
No matter the religion and drives
Us as well as them into endless wars.

When we do the right thing according
To this tradition, religion or way
In which we were brought up we
Gain strength and fortitude in doing
What we know to be correct.
                                  This
Certitude has made for martyrs in
Every part of the world as well as for
The dedication of lives to service
And the comforting of others.
                                 Poverty
And humility are also golden tokens
Of belief and a Poor Clare or a Monk
Begging in the street in Katmandu
All are supported by their faiths that
Serve them so well they continue
To smile as they suffer the world.

Faith is a luxury and as such
It makes for strength and courage
More than any other single thing in life.

Winter Solstice III

This is the time when the great wheel
Of the year dips down
When the sun shines the trees
In the north at noon
When the deer's breath and the hare's breath
And the dog's cloud are still cold
With their small handfuls of steam
This is the time when the cross exists
Only in the outstretched arms
Of the winter's tree
And the child in each of us is born once more.

This is the time when the great wheel
Of the world dips down
When the wave's spume becomes ice
As the wind takes the salt drops to give them shape
For a moment before
Dropping them once again
Into the hard driving sea to melt,
This is the time when so many of those
Ready to die choose to go
Into the space between the stars
Where the dreams live
And the child in each of us is born once more.

This is the time when the great wheel
Of the stars dips down
When the Pleiades come close
And the Great Bear shines
When the summer's fruit
And the winter's grain join
In the faith that Spring will come
And be light again.
This is the time that forgives the hurt
That sings and praises
And the child in each of us is born once more.

Wondering

Dante's ability to keep on writing
His terzine describing his improbable voyage
To Hell and back while he suffered
The pains of creditors, of exile and of
The disruption of his family's life
Teaches all of us a lesson in the way
One must learn to live several lives
At the same time.
                        Almost as if we
Were living a life in a big highrise
Of the mind with several floors
Stacked one upon another with one roof
One foundation and an elevator
To take us up and down stopping
At various floors as our particular
Buttons keep being pushed to send
Us busily traveling up and down
With hardly any time at all
Between floors to pause and rest.

Strange how we have evolved
To be living many more than
One life at a time while still
Preparing for our singular
Mortality.

To Live With The Beloved

To live with the beloved
One does not rely solely
On mystic connections
The alembic dance of the flowers
The understandings of never before
The sweat of delight in the bed
The stillness of sunset
When the wind has died down
And there is food in the house.

To live with the beloved
One does not leap into
Dangerous waters, quicksand
Or otherwise risk life and soul
Without concern, play cards
With the devil, give up
Discourse, run with the crowd,
Retire into deserts and solitude
Or bark at the moon dismayingly.

To live with the beloved
One must learn to be up
With the dawn for its blessings
To wash dishes as sacrament
To clean the house in ways
That are luminous, to sing
And fetch and follow through and
Tend to the tangible maintaining
The body in balance with spirit.

Otherwise the days are numbered, the sand
Is measured out, the fabric tears, expressions
Ring hollow, the bud withers
And one is no longer there
At all.

For Alexander

From your earliest days in Sausalito
Walking on that deck framed by trees
Your eyes always stretched to the horizon
And that horizon has shifted so many times
And so many ways since then.
                                  Bicycling over the Himalayas
Then exploring the mysteries of Vietnam after
That war had its way you have always
Seen various levels on which the world
Chooses to show itself and it is not only your eye
But your ear that has become sensitive
To the intonations of problems and solutions.

You create worlds of your own from Hong Kong
To Chamonix, from California to Mexico and
Then sharing them all with us so that
We all are better in our knowledge and
Our spirit because of your sharing.

You and Flora have managed to manage
The requirements of two cultures in tandem
Not without some confrontations but in the main
With a joining together of disparate elements
To make a symphony of feelings and of light.

Your life does sing and as you keep on
Traveling I see how you are constantly
Weaving a tapestry that will be admired
But more importantly will manage
To present to all who care who we are.

To My Daughter Romana

The glowing embers in the fire bowl
Are brilliantly red in their darkness.
The memories of loving your mother
Seem to have found their place
In the world of today, the one
She left four years ago
                              Or
Was it five? Too long in any way
And in this electronic world
Of immediate transmissions
I thank you my daughter
For this image you sent
Because it was the trigger
That shot open the images
Of that great life we all
Had together in that time
In California now
So long ago.

For Gavilan

Down to the lower pasture
The one by the river this morning
To say goodbye to Gavilan today
Because sick and old at twenty two
His legs having given all their strength
To him and his riders for these many,
These 88 seasons, carrying us up and
Down our trails, our mountains, quietly,
Gently, knowing when to move out and
When to stay, having been part of the herd,
The family, the tribe all these years
Now in pain with every step, eye still
Quiet and gentle, reaching head high
To the hand he knows not knowing
Tomorrow will be his last full day
And the day after just a short one
To be cut short by the Vet and his crew
Who will come to put him down, send
Him to horse heaven to ride free out
In the sky joining the sparrow hawks
He was named after to then
Be buried down by the Bosque
Down by the riverbank near the trail
Where we rode together for so many years
And now that I too am sore in the legs
And know that there is a time for all of
Us to be and then to become part of
The sky, someone's memory, history
Or even of the wind as it blows down
The lower pasture to take him away.

The Practice Of Sacrifice
—for a friend on the occasion
of her double mastectomy

At Delphi they would bring myrtle and oranges
And sweets and clay and silver offerings giving
Thanks for their futures. At Eleusis they would
Bring their questions and their hopes and dreams
As well as olive branches and cattle for the
Priestesses. At Carthage, in the temples, they
Would even bring their first born and snuff them
And leave them in little jars and boxes.

In Tenochtitlan, at the altars on the pyramids, the
Priests would tear out the hearts of prisoners in the
Name of flowers. In the Andes they would
Crush the skulls of young girls dressed for the
Occasion leaving their bodies with offerings in the
Mountain ice. In Spain the pyres of the Inquisition
Charred enough bodies and spirit to merit many
Interesting chapters in the Book of Religions.
In Salem, Mass., they burned witches as sacrifices
For the good of the Commonwealth. In Vietnam
54,000 of ours and millions of theirs were sacrificed
To a vision as stupid as there ever has been, not to
Mention the Holocaust and the Gulag and the Tai
Ping rebellion and all those killed for reasons of color.
Or the Big One, that of Christ, done first on Calvary
And still now, daily, again and again, all over the world.

While today, in America, the breasts of old and
Young women, of beautiful and plain ones, of rich
And poor ones are cut off daily to save their lives,
Their images and their marriages without even a prayer
Or incense on the altar to justify the practice of sacrifice
To stave Death off once again.

Even In Winter

Open your hearts
Let the sun stream in
In spite of everyday troubles
In spite of disappointments
In spite of car wrecks, debts
And disasters.

Nourish Hope.

The one that keeps one going.
Be kind to yourself and, yes,
Do open your hearts,
So that love may enter
And dance your desires
Even in winter.

Open your hearts.

Let the sun stream in
Each day is a wonder
If only we let it become
The bringer of pleasures
To all those you love
And to those who love you
Even in winter

Timor Mortis

Those trees are so stark
Against the grey Sunday afternoon
December sky seeming to be angry
And distraught with no leaf
Left on those branches clawing
The air in desperation.
                      Difficult
To believe that Spring will come
To bring the green back to them
This time around and that
The Summer that is to come
Will have them singing with
The birds and with ourselves
Again.
          Wondering at times
If this last summer was
Indeed the last time these
Trees would leaf out and
Live!
         Timor Mortis conturbat me!
The fear of death
Troubles me as I see the trees
Wondering if they will indeed
Return to green.

When One Is Chosen

Having been reminded once again
That it is Love that chooses one and
That no matter how one tries
No one, no person can choose Love,
Ever, in any way at all.
                        Yes, there
Are those who will, by default, accept
A Semblance, a Relation or Partnership
A Chord of Comfort, of Social Being,
Or even a Paid For Companionship
In Love's place and there are also those
Who, having failed once and tried
And failed again give up altogether
And turn to other things in life
Learning to live without Love.
                             But any
One who ever has been chosen
Is changed and becomes a carrier
Of the Light that is bestowed
When Love chooses one.
                          And then there
Are times when one is in the orchard
And picks a ripe peach off its bough
Biting into its soft sweet flesh
With pleasure and a smile, not
Realizing that it was that one branch
With that one ripe peach that picked
The picker rather than the other way
Around.

Duende

Some have found it
Between the demon and the angel
Others in a lover's look
And yet others in a song
Impossible to translate

It slides between the gypsy's legs
And keeps on dancing
Even in disaster times
Good and bad times
And the death of friends
Settled somewhere between
Surprise and surfeit
It establishes its own rhythm
And demands attention
While rushing by on the wings
Of a hawk or falcon
It is a thing
Or an expression
Or a feeling all its own

It evokes a sense of loss
At the same time as the sense
Of discovery
              It makes one sigh
Or cry, depending on the moment,
And embraces fate
All on its own.

Repetition

How many times do we have to do it?

In Rome several times, in France
There was the French Revolution
In Russia the Bolshevik one
And now do we have to do
The American one to change it
To change the system which holds
The 1% at the top with all they have
And the rest barely making it
From day to day and year to year
Call it Capitalism if you will
Or call it another betrayal.

It's the Feast in the House of Buffet
Or Rockefeller or Bloomberg or the NYSE
Before the days of revenge once again.

Yes, once again, with banks and palaces
And monetary markets destroyed and
With everyone scrambling for a piece
Of that which seems stable.
How many times do the rich have to pay
For their riches, their holdings?

The clock of history makes its turns
And when it is due to strike, it will.

And how long it will take to break
The status quo or the world markets?

It will be a question until it happens
And when it does and the world
Picks up the pieces once again
And summarily starts rebuilding
For expectations this time will certainly
Be different and we start again.

Question

What do you do when the day arrives
That you recognize the bifurcation in your lives
What you do as a poet makes perfect sense
But you also have to do what makes dollars & cents.

They say it takes 20 pennies to make a dime these days
And economics continues incessantly to amaze
But when one is still working for one's daily bread
While sweating one's way with one's daily dread
It makes one want to give up one or the other.

And in the end one asks why does one bother
To be a poet. One is not bound nor even free
To feel great for a moment and then stupid
But then an angel always comes by
And hits you on the head right out of the sky
And you are made to wonder again and again
What made you choose such a difficult strain
And not finding the answer in all your tries
You continue in your work maintaining surprise
Without which there would never be poetry of any kind
And all poets like Homer would end up blind
So let me stop this questioning ramble
Because if I did not is would be a shamble
And I never learned to lean on the door
As I found my way out of this room
To the sounds of the cannons going "boom"
In my head realizing I never should have said
I was a poet in the first place before I was dead.

Lonely

And finally it gets down to the point
Where there is no one left to speak with
About those other days when you met
Your children's mother or when you took
Your father's ashes out to sea or when
You closed your first major transaction
Or even when you moved into your
First home in Sausalito or the one at
Stinson Beach — yes you can always
Tell the stories but there is no one
Left to say "yes, and" and then
Continue it.
           No one with whom
The making of those stories was shared
And then you know you are as
Alone as one can be living with
Memories.
           And then one day
A book arrives and you are afraid
To do anything but fish in it
Because you've opened it here and
There and suddenly surprises
Have jumped out to bite you
And you look at the index
And there are still things
Waiting for you so you go
Ahead and close it so that
You may have something
To look forward to, you know
You will be sharing something
That will surprise you so as
To make you feel alone but in
A better way.

Earnings

Call it what you will
Reward for hard work
Accumulation of land, of wealth
Security in the middle of trouble
Build your safe place, castle,
County or tower with a moat
Around it to make it defensible
It still will come down
When the time comes and the crowds
Will just make themselves manifest
Stirring and jostling and crying
Out loud "enough!" and "enough!"

We've had enough and things
Have to change today
Not tomorrow, today and
You may want to label the time
The movement, the attitude
But the labels won't matter
With social media now giving
Us all a way to be with
Each other, instantly
As never before, to use the knife,
The cane, the club, or even
A piece of wood to claim
Your share before it's too late
And your children's share
Before anyone else takes it
Away once again.   The name
Does not matter Capitalism
Money, Treasure, Riches,
When one has
More than anyone else
Which still ends up with
The problems of having, owning
And always wanting something more.

A Comfort Zone

A church, a temple, a meeting place
Where people gather to be together
In the name of this god or saint or
Spirit defines the need we all have
To belong.
          To belong to a congregation
All of whose members have chosen
A way of looking at the world
In the same way makes for comfort.
Children are born into the beliefs of parents
And when the parents die they do so
Still within the same system
Of belief that guided them during
Their lives.
          This sense of belonging
Makes for comfort not only in the now
Of life but also in terms of that
Which is beyond, when we as humans
Die.

And there are ceremonies that tie
All of us together from baptism at birth
To the incantations that facilitate
Our dying.
          Since time began we all
Have chosen this way of guarding
Our loneliness, our individuality
By joining hands and building
Cathedrals, towers and even country churches
Synagogs and temples
To be together.

For Papa

Daring to toss traditions and even pieces
Of your heritage for the love of your life,
For the one who became your wife and
Mother of your children — always brave
In confronting the many challenges
That confronted you in terms of beliefs,
Of military orders and civic obligations,
Standing properly positioned with the other
Foreign officers along with the Chinese ones,
Bemedaled, brave in each case. You taught
Us to stand without flinching no matter
The circumstances, ready to move on.

And when the time came to diminish
The arc of your life you taught us that
Even the fitting of ships and the selling of wine
Could be done in ways that did not diminish
Who you were and what you lived for.

You taught us to look into the Divine Comedy,
Into the sayings of Mencius and Confucius
As well as the plays of Shakespeare and
The work of Michelangelo and even that of
D'Annunuzio, the glories of Venice and the ties
To Torcello the family had had.

In your last days as alone as anyone could be
With your wife and your children already
Mourning your passing you stood firm, as the
Grim reaper came calling. We took your ashes
Out into the Golden Gate that you had
Made possible for us and found your spirit
Still with us on our return to shore.

For Mami

Irrepressible in your ability to see the good and
To be responsible for all the care you gave us
Always ready to defend us, your children,
Or the friends you had made in the many worlds
You visited while being our father's loving wife
As well as the caring mother of our lives.
                                                                        Today
To celebrate your birth oh those many years ago
You, who always managed to find the right words,
And who are still alive in the memories and
In the conscious lives of your children continue
To shape the way the world is for us while
Still reminding us of all the lives and places
We came from.
                             Those four young Scots heading out
To Jerusalem in the first crusade, the woman painter
At the court of the King of Spain, the grandfather
Who dared to begin the undoing of the Empire
Of the Ottomans as well as well as the other aunt
Who served the nuns who served their congregations
In Europe and in Asia all woven into the story
Of our family by you who taught us how to be
Worthy of all that came before while dealing
With all the challenges of our futures.
                                                     We,
Your four children, honor you by doing the best
We know how to do, carrying your caring thoughts
Into our futures with the kind of loving care
You gave us as we grew up within the armature
Of your loving arms....brave and beautiful always.

This One Is For Yanko Varda

Descended from the clouds
Thou master of colour and of grace
Have arrived in order teach us
The attributes of the open heart.

We have been blessed by your appearance
And you have made us look deep into
Our very beings to find all that is not worthy
Of the happy and beautiful life
And to throw it out and away
So as to permit Joy and Colour and Grace
And all the loveliness in the world
To become manifest in your people.

Yes, we are your people, you who have taught us
To be generous and concurrently to treasure
Each moment, each wave crashing on the shore,
Each raindrop and all the colours of the universe.

With you we are more alive each moment
More aware of the different aspects of these
Moments and grateful that we are alive
To sing and paint and sail with you
Into the awareness of this world which you
Have made more rich and generous than any other

All praise and gratitude from our open hearts.
All joy and song and laughter as you
Master of Masters have come to be with us.

Sausalito 1968

Money

We have become so tied to it
That knowing if and when it's coming
Or even if it will be there at all
Determines how we feel, how we are
Even with our closest relatives and
Even what our blood pressure
Is going to be until we know.

There was a time when being
In a state of grace having
All one's sins forgiven was enough
To make one feel at one with all
The world and every one we knew.
Now it seems that knowing how
The banker at the till feels today
About one's very own accounts means
More than any other blessing
One could have.   That a medium
Of exchange could become itself
A quotient of one's feelings seems
Ridiculous but our society's turned
Into a counting house in which
One's worth is only measured by
That which one has in hand or yet
To come for sure.   A sad commentary
On all the strides the human mind
Has made in understanding this world,
This universe and even its own kind.

It's how much you have in the bank
How much is yet to come and when
That is the question put now even by
Lovers who have just met as well as
By those you have lived with for what
Could be mistaken for all your life.

The Illusion Of Control

Came out of the caves, did we?
Having controlled fire so as to eat
What did not feed us when it was raw
Meat, grain, green things making
Us separate and distinct from animals,
Knowing we could control our hungers
And we did until excess, greed, lust
All those illusions came to tame us.

We then built empires, vast armies
That empowered us to rule over others
From the earliest recorded times from
Egyptian, Roman view points and also
From those of Genghis Khan and those
Others who sent fleets to discover
New continents and their gold thus
Feeding again the illusion of control.

So, now, having landed on the Moon
And aiming still to get to Mars quite soon
We choose to ignore the troubles here
On Earth, that should have been named
Water, while strutting about as we
Are wont to do when empowered
Believing once again that Control
Is in fact ours.   List them if you will
From Solomon to the Ptolemies, from
The Caesars to the Emperors and then
To the Napoleons, the Mussolinis,
Hitlers and Stalins of mixed memory
To the Khadaffis and Obamas
Each one manifesting that singular
Timeless and dangerous illusion
Whose ramifications always manifest
Deaths, famines and the extinction
Of hopes nourished on hard work
And the greening of the seasons.

Not Good Enough

Talk about Armageddon and the Apocalypse,
Did it not all start here at Trinity about
One Hundred and Ten Miles south of us
Before Hiroshima, Nagasaki, Fukushima
And that plant in California that was
Just shut down?
                      Discussions still continue as
To how we should interpret the Mayan Calendar
And its version of the End of Time and the way
In which the Rapture will lift some of us
Sky high while leaving all the rest of us to die.

Dante in his Divine Comedy described with grand
Authority the many kinds of Hell and the Mountain
Of Purgatory before revealing the Paradise of
Eternal Light so that Believers from then on, down
To our day would have a map to travel by, while
Some non believers still believe that Moses
Was the Pharaoh's Daughter's Son and not a Jew
At all who had learned magic and how to part
The waters when he had been just a boy at court.

Yes Trinity and Eternity and the Pitts still being made
Just up the Hill from us all factor into an equation
That can turn our Planet into just another cinder
In the sky which is not an argument good enough
To have us abandon civility and do nothing but
Just give up and then lie down and die.

Easter Morning

When the stone was rolled away He strode into the light
And thanked the Angels who had come to help, and then
He saw Mary from Magdala, disconsolate, coming up the hill
To be with Him once more.
They embraced as they had done before.
Then He showed himself to Thomas and to Matthew
And later, to Peter, to Levi and to the others.
                                                Belief becomes
The clothing we wear for comfort.
                                    Believing in the Resurrection
And the Life makes it possible for us to endure, even to the death
The most terrible of tortures, as He did, when crucified, and
When, out of that sacrifice, so many interpretations came to be,
That their variety has now caused more deaths than any plague
While so many of us still want to believe and pray while
Acknowledging the Truth
As well as the Illusion for the rest of us.
                                        It is Spring,
And we do find so many ways of acknowledging the turning
Of the Season, the tipping of the Planet's crown so as to
Celebrate the arrival of new leaves and grass with ceremonies
And pleasures.
                    We laugh and dance and sing and decorate
The eggs we fetch which we then hide and seek and find.
We celebrate the fertility of rabbits, invoke Pan with flutes
And manage the eagerness of Spring so as not to disturb
The balance of the world.
                            We do all this as greed and malice
Continue to spill blood in useless sacrifice in Israel, in Gaza,
In Afghanistan, Iraq and Chechnya as it has been spilled
In Indonesia, Rwanda and Kosovo,
And yet the Sun this Spring
Continues to bring light out of the shadows,
Out of the dark of tombs and into the Song
Of being alive and well, filled with Hope again,
Not only in terms of this life of ours but in terms
Of all the generations yet to come.

Sea Song

We came here by sea
Driven by the winds of circumstance
To find new lives to be built out
Of the many storied wreckage
Of our pasts.
               Yes, those pasts that reach
Back to the time when we were
Minor priests in the Temple in Jerusalem
Until it became necessary for us to flee
Into Egypt, into those deserts
As it is said the Holy Family had fled,
But they returned, as History recites
And we did not, but kept on going
Across the top of Africa until
We were confronted by the rocks
That to those day guard the way
Out into the ocean to remind us
Of Ulysses and his crew who left
No trace behind.
               But we crossed North
And went on beyond the coastal ranges
To find work and futures once again
Before going on to Genoa and Venice
Once the Sovereigns of Spain had
Pronounced the reasons for another Exodus
And so went from Spain to Italy
With our histories and then later
Into China until arriving here in California
More than halfway around this planet
We have arrived with appreciation
At this beautiful place
We have learned to call home.

Yes, we did come here by sea with histories
Of service in recent wars that touched on
The beginning of the undoing of that empire
Of the Ottomans that had held a good part
Of the known world in thrall for centuries
And from there to parse the history
Of what the wars at sea are like.

From the Red Sea to the Pacific
To the return to this new country of ours
To sing songs and discover islands
Of fascination as people we came to know
And work with built structures in this area
That have lasted and will last beyond
Our current lives, giving our children
And theirs an indication that to serve
And to be loyal are as important
As bread and wine and poetry and laughter
Are to the well being of each one of us.

Fortunate in having found teachers from whom
We have learned to see around corners
To hear in the silences of the night
And to continue to sail around the world
Without leaving our beds until dawn comes.
                                        In time
I am certain that one of us will weave a cloth
Out of all our histories, the ones mentioned and
All the others, Vikings, Scots, teachers, and traders
And this cloth will be an ensign to show
That if we choose we can live good lives and
Build delight for all of us as my brother Mark
Has done with his sculputures that delight
The world as they weave the light
Around our eyes and sing.

The Adriatic

Knowing this sea to have been Hadrian's
As much as the wall that still stands between
Those Scotsmen and the Brits
                                       This sea that became
The Mare Nostrum, Our Sea, known as the Sea of
Adria, becoming the Adriatic for all of us who
Have shared in some way with those fortunes
Made and lost while traveling or fighting,
Venice and Constantinople,
Battles like Lepanto and cities
That became fortresses or the other way around.
                                                                         Now
Sun drenched with white houses looking like sheep
From a distance, crowding the shore, the bay, any
Old or new place to make a landing, a stop for water
And perhaps discovering another treasure for the trove.

Was it not Curzzola, now Korcula, where Marco Polo
Was born? So the legends say while the sun
Still sits up in the blue as if it had always known
Where it belonged and the legendary stories
Tell us all once again that this sea belongs
To us and we always have been part of it.

A Chance Meeting

I have just met the Angel of Death
She is sweet and charming
And not at all as scary
As we have all been
Brought up to think. No,
She is gentle and comforting,
Works a lot in hospices
And sees that tender care becomes
Available when necessary.
                    Really caring,
She is there to hold your hand and to
Comfort you when you are about to leave.

All those frightening stories about Death
Coming as a skeleton in the cart of death
To tear your life away are just there
To get you to say prayers and to give
Your goods to some cause or other.
                                But
No, she is there to ease your passing,
To hold you when you need to be held
And to tell you the world will go on
When you yourself are gone.
                        She is
Even there when there is an accident,
A car crash or when a plane falls
Out of the sky and, though busy,
She tells me she is always there
For every single one of us.
                        It's her job,
She said, as she smiled and reached
Out to touch my hand recently.

For All Of Us

This was the sea once, and I walk across the hills,
Down to the arroyo and up again with my eyes
Swimming across the face of a blind escarpment,
Seeing red and ochre bluffs as some strange
Finned creature must have eyed them
When all was water here instead of air and
Another way of being was the way.

I think of that reptilian ancestor whose appetite
For light drove him and his kind to breathe air,
Instead of water. They took possession of the
Land wondering if there was another way to be.

I know that when my children first saw the light
They came out of that same sea and their children
Too, in turn, will rise from there into the air
With perhaps a better chance of finding still
Another way.

This was the sea once and the sun rests on solstice
Night while the midsummer dark is forked
By lightning that charges down the draw,
Driving the huge and crackling thunder into the
Ground reminding us once more that all things
Change, some slowly, and others in a flash.
Always another way to be.

The Two Cousins

Time and love are kin. Both are intangible
And yet touch and shape each and every thing
We do. Each stretches out to distances unseeable
While holding within themselves the power to bunch up,
Creating chaos in their folds as in this piece of
Crumpled paper. Yes, each one lives in all we do
And becomes even more noticeable when either leaves
Our lives and disappears.
                              When time stops for us, we die.
When love stops we may not die immediately, but often
Wish we had.
However, when time sings for us and all
Its moves are somersaults of bright delight, it's really quite
The same as when we fall in love, head over heels in love,
Heeding the gentle push that nature gives us when we see
A candidate, a likely mate with whom we'd make
A perfect child — and odd how we think it's our free
Will at work when it's only the old wise Mother
Saying, "Yes, that one would do for you" — and then,
There is the time for it, the time that makes it happen

Dance, sing, and play while one loses all sense of time,
Discovering the pleasures of forevers.

They are indeed kin to each other, these two. They
Frame the world in which you and I can be together;
Lose one, and you've lost the other.

Riff #10
About A Woman

Not about any woman, and yet about all women,
At the same time, so that they can and will and do,
Become that woman, who is that woman who fulfills, filling
The whole world so full, it spills right over into beauty with
Breath and breadth, as bounty to bless and justify, the
Existence of all the saints of all religions making out of the
Fiction of heaven, tangible reality....That woman for whom
All the plays have been written, produced, performed,
Perceived and praised, and damned as well. That woman who
Is herself, without youth or age, who is there when while
Giving, receives, remembers, and retrieves with hope, even for
Those without hope, all of the helpless....The one whose
Name is both, Mary and Maria, whose name is Kwan Yin as
Well as Isis, and Astarte, and Andromeda, as well the one who
Shares, shines, and sparkles while furnishing reasons to build
The house, light the fire, plow the fields, put out to sea,
Haul the nets in, and soar into the sky, while she trusts,
Believes, has confidence, and faith in the outcome. She is that
Very one whose thought becomes arrow and target, both at the
Same time, instant and second, who holds the universe in
Balance and beauty, becoming laughter and lightness, singing
In the light of the dawn before sunrise. That woman who is
Sister of your own heart's self, while also Lilith at the identical
Moment, apricot-skinned, sweet, and salt sweated, at the same
Time, in whom trust and reverence rise, as if summoned by
Star or by Reason. That one again, who measures eternity in an
Instant, and light years with her outstretched arm, who is as
Gentle as cats are — at evening light....Woman of clouds, of
Wind and of salt spume, the one you have known and loved
And been with, without knowing her, without being fully
Aware of her marrow, her scent, her knees and divisions. She is
That one woman who becomes song in the quiet of dusk, and
Is also the stamping of feet on floors that clack and resound,
With the chords of guitars, and the clapping and clicking and
Laughter and challenge of fingers and thumbs snapping.

While becoming tambourine, castanet, ring cymbal and drum,
Flirting with brilliance and sparkles and the bang and slap of
Heels, brought sharp to the floor with a crack, echoing the
Snap of the whip, of the cape, of the fist brought hard into
Palm and the toe tapping, drumming. While she comes out of
The dark into the beam of light shining again, becoming
Moth, dream, memory and vengeance, who is out and about,
The touch of thigh, touched by thigh, of hands touching hips,
Of flesh and of home lost, and alone in the night,
Frightened of phantasm who drift in unannounced, ready to
Pounce and devour. What she is about, this woman, who
Suddenly turns away becoming like ice as defense because the
Color is wrong or the lamp is not right or the paint is still wet
And the bet has been lost and no matter the cost she turns and
We go, no we run, no we fly after her to say that it was all a
Mistake, a fault in the doing, the reason for undoing all the
Plans, so that in fact, the boat was missed but we got to port
Somehow because she is what she is about. This woman who
Sings in the morning and touches herself with the pleasures of
Feathers and sunlight of dawning and dreaming this one who
Is all mother and sister and daughter and daughter and sister
And mother in turn who turns into gentle and sweetness and
Caring while also daring to turn into star flesh and firelight
And the dancing of waters, of swallows at evening and of
Finches at dawning as the sun rises and shines its way into
Corners that had been hidden, rushing the dark light for all of
Us as only she has ever known how she who is there when
She's needed, who is offered the world as a token of all the
Great treasures within it, who is given the rainbow as a token
Of color, and of all that is yet to be found, becoming aware
That she is both a part and a party to all that is pleasure…
Triune in her measures, with Spirit and wisdom and body all
Present, who sings and who listens, who writes and who reads,
Who caresses the breeze of desire as well as the one of
Jaguar and the song of the thrush, always ready to find and to
Be found, unclothed, waiting for the caress of the beloved
While caressing him, who teaches by being and is at the same
Time, herself, the teaching, the dance, the music, the starlight

And dew, while all the while she who is the other part of my
Heart and its beating, the breath of my lung and my skin's own
Touch. This woman who is herself and no other, not even
Similar to all of the others I had loved before, almost as
Practice for this time, this moment, this touch of the sun's
Traveling, with its rays breaking through clouds on their way
To the Piñon, as the mountains rise to give it good fortune so
That this woman rises again each day with the dawning, with
Feathers, with touching, with all that is there in the world
Because this woman is about learning and teaching and
Feasting and fasting and dancing and falling and rising as the
Wings of the eagle that touch you and hold you as you fly over
Mountains...and also about her inventions, her treasures and
Laughter and also about the calm that pervades her, the one
That makes sleeping beside her the rest of all time, the one
Who wakes you with teasing and softness, who is all that she
Is because she is that one who is.

At La Villita

In this place of quiet, by the river, green,
A thousand miles from the nearest sea
Where kind and gentle care kept him
From dying as so many of his like had done
Out of drink, despair, betrayals and even war
Where he was comforted in spite of ways
Which were not the ones he had been born
To live; he found himself repeatedly facing
The surge of ocean in dreams, in visions
Along with the grace of gulls and dolphins
As he learned to live a life with horses,
Eagles, coyotes and with cats and dogs along
With mountain men and women who had
Never even seen the sea but had heard of it.

Blending trust with gratitude, he would
Find ways from time to time to taste
The salt air at dawn, hear the wave's slap
And flinch once more as the wind at the bow
Would burn his face and eyes on lookout.

It was not his youth he wanted back, not
The ability to move with sea bag upon shoulder
Down to shipping hall and the unknown beyond
But the sea itself that covers so much
More than half of our planet's skin that kept
Calling him back to that Republic of Ocean
In which the Sacred Islands shape hearts
And feelings without boundaries, without signs
That proclaim "Private Property—Do Not Enter."

We all were born in that sea which filled
Our mothers' wombs before we came out
To breathe air as we have learned to do
Among all the other things we've learned;
And so many of us seem to be inured
To the sea's call, to its demands and disciplines
That we forget that place we all came from

Which is still our destination even though
So many of us live in mountain meadows.
                                                          We
Rush through city streets and continue to engage
Our lives in growing crops, in doing business and
Driving ourselves and others down the freeways
While going about the work of wars of one kind
Or another in the names of Liberty and Peace.

The tides still rise and fall in daily certainty
And the whales and dolphins still breathe air
After having gone back to the sea after their time
As mammals on these lands, and now, with
The Global Warming of this small planet on which
We live he wonders how long before the sea
Will come once again to claim its shores.
                                                          He knows
It will not be long after he will have gone, and
Still it amuses him to think how much more
In the way of violence takes place on land
Than in the stretches of the Ocean that his kind
Has always known to be the better place to be.

That place of long horizons and dreams
Where one can be one with one another and
With the stars, their constellations, their ways
And the thousand million nebulae that are the Universe
So that we may eventually learn to know the wellness
That winds and dark ocean depths can give to us.

Autumn Leaves

The golden leaves falling from the cottonwoods
Make a carpet around the last brave roses
That have managed to keep some color
Of their own in their red and orange petals
That survived the first frosts of the year.

The richness of the remaining green
With all the autumn colors sing a song
Of summer memories and of cold to come.

A time of beauty that is both a time
Of loss and of new promises.
       We are
Fortunate to be the point between
The past and all
That is still to come.

Summer's gone, Autumn's here
Harvest time before cold Winter
Comes down to the fields.
       Stillness
In the air. The world is waiting
And all that has to be done
Is being done one day at a time.

The leaves give the sun back
Its color as they fall golden
To the ground.
      The trees know
That in the Spring there will
Be new ones to bring green
Back into the light before
We will see their gold again.

A pigeon came to sit on the head of St. Francis
There, the statue on the west side of the garden.
They both seemed to smile for a moment
Then the bird had other things to do

And left and it really seemed that St. Francis
Turned his head up and to the left
For just a moment.
                    Then the wind came up,
A few more leaves fluttered down the golden day
And all went back to be just as it had been before.

It really depends on the yardstick
That is used to determine the length
Of anything, a smile, a life, some silk
Or even cotton, a marriage and even
An absence.
                    Choose your own carefully
Before determining the length of anything.

In a country run by thieves the rich
Are honored, cared for, protected
Because, if not, there would be
Not much left to steal.
                    This runs so
Long as things don't get too much
Out of hand.

Are They The Same?

In Spanish
I want you
And
I love you
Use the same words.

Yo te quiero, y
Yo te quiero
Are the same words

In no other language
That I know
Is it put so clearly

And are they really
The same or are they
Equivalent in other
Ways?
        Wanting
And loving — are they
The two sides of the coin?
Or is one a reflection
Of the other?
        Today
And every day I wake
I ask myself to take
Another look to see
Whether they are the same
In Spanish or in any
Other tongue.

The Same Thing

It is the same thing that drives the stallion
To mount the willing mare standing there
In the meadow winking and waving her tail
As if to say "I'm here for you, big boy."

The same thing that drove Mark Anthony and
Caesar to want the power of Empire so as to have
That which each one wanted —
                              The same thing
That drove Henry the Eighth into those paroxysms
Of lust and fury that divided England from Rome —
Always the same down to our time when
Another King of England threw his Empire to the wind
For the whetting of his appetites —
                                    We are an odd lot
Inventing grand towering names for that feeling
That comes over us as it came over King David
When he saw Bathsheba bathing on her roof
That summer's afternoon not so long ago
Causing murder and betrayal in the palace.

It's the same thing that's made women careless
And men foolish since it all began, yes, the same
Thing that moves the finches and the other
Birds to build their nests in Spring — that makes
The white tailed doe stand quivering in Autumn
In the high meadows of this mountain range.
The same thing that fuels all the attention given
To the development of abs and quads in health clubs
Across the country and the marketing of creams,
Of clothes, of perfumes and of dreams so as to enhance
The desirability of each and every one of us.

What Is Your Name?

Who are you,
Saint of the near miss, the close call?
Turning the car's wheel
Deflecting the knife's point
So that we walk out of the hospital
The next day greeting the sun
Gratefully?

What are you, guardian angel,
Kachina, invisible spirit and friend,
You — the one who makes the judge
Hear our side of the case, who drops
The name from the list,
Wakes the lookout on time
And makes one miss the train
That connected with the plane that goes down?

I build you this poem at dawn
Gratefully listening to the squawking of jays,
To the sound of water falling
And to the intermittent silence
Wondering how it is that so few
Know you, acknowledge you, praise you,
Saint of the near miss, the close call.

¿Cuál es Tu Nombre?

¿Qué én eres tú,
Santo del casi y del por poco?
¿Dándole vuelta a la rueda del carro,
Desviando la punta del cuchillo
Para que salgamos del hospital
El siguiente día a saludar al sol
Llenos de gracia?
¿Qué eres tú, un Angel de la Guarda,
Kachina, un espíritu invisible y amigo,
Tú — él que hace que el juez
Escuche nuestreo caso, él que
Quita el nombre de la lista,
Y despierta al centinela a la hora
Y que hace que uno pierda el tren
¿Que connectaba con el aveón que se va para abajo?
Te construyo este poema al alba
Agradecido escuchando a los arrandejos granar
Al sonido de la caída del agua
Y el silencio intermitente
Preguntándome cómo es que son tan pocos
Los que te conocen, te han visto, te han venerado,
Santo del casi y el por poco.

We Do Not Own

You don't own the four directions child,
They own you. The mountain owns you.
The meadows by the river, fringed and tasseled
By the cottonwoods, own you. The bluffs
In the barrancas you see when you look north,
Own you. Even the arroyo owns you.
You, child, are theirs. You belong to them.
Someone, somewhere, that first day of fences
Said "mine" and said "for my children,"
And then it grew and grew and counties
Became states and became nations
And Cain and Abel's story kept on being
Taught because it made us righteous
In the land — that's really where it all began.
First slings, then bows and arrows
And then the guns — until we broke the
Atom up to make sure no one else could
Or would find a way to breach our walls,
Still forgetting we do not own a thing.
Child, the deer knows the way, so does Coyote.
They know where the seasons take them;
They know where the wind comes from
And where it goes. Even Raven plays
Those currents in the air we cannot see.
And yet each one of them knows home —
The matted corner in the meadow, the den
Scooped out of sandstone cliff, the dark
Nests in the arms of trees all say
This is the place of rest for them.
Taste all the distances you need, explore
The gorges, discover roadways made of dreams,
But be ready when the time comes, to say
This is the place in which to rest,
The place to be, knowing you will not
Ever own it if you count on staying free.

No Somos Los Dueños

Tú no eres el dueño de las cuatro direcciones niño,
Tú les perteneces. Le perteneces a las montañas.
Los campos al lado del rio, bordeados y adornados con borlas
De Alamos, son tu dueño. Los riscos
En las barrancas que tEu ves cuando miras al norte,
Son tu dueño. Y hasta el arroyo te posee.
Tú, niño, eres de ellos. Tú les perteneces.
Alguien, en algún lugar en ese primer día de cercos
Dijo "mio" y dijo "por mis hijos,"
Y luego creció y los paises
Se hicieron estados y se convirtieron en naciones
Y la historia de Cain y Abel su fué
Enseñando para hacernos sentir justos
En la tierra—así fué como realmente todo
Emprezó, primero las resorteras y el arco y la flecha
Y después las armas—hasta que quebrantamos
El átomo para aseguaranos de que nadie má pudiera
Encontrar la forma de romper nuestras murallas
Y aún continuamos oldándonos que no poseemos nada.
Niño, el venado sabe el camino, y también el coyote.
Ellos saben a donde los llevan las estaciones;
Ellos saben de donde viene el viento
Y a donde va. Y hasta Cuervo juega
Con esas corrientes en el aire que nosotros no podemos ver.
Y aún así cada uno de ellos sabe su hogar —
El rincón enmarañado en la pradera, la madriguera
Excavada del peñasco arenizo, los oscuros
Nidos en los brazos de los árboles todos dicen
Este es el lugar de descanso para ellos.
Prueba todas las distancias que necesites, explora
Los desfiladeros, descubre los caminos hechos de sueños,
Pero estéte listo cuando el tiempo llegue para decir
Este es el lugar en el cual se descansa
El lugar para ser, sabiendo que tú nunca lo
Poseerás si cuentas con quedarte libre.

Rediscovering Books On A Shelf

I find myself reading Poetry these days as if I had already died
And returned for an hour or so to get back to those shelves
Where I had filed so many of those books that had taught me
To think, to see, to sing and to cry as well as to pray
From time to time.
                    Not only the Commedia and the work
Of friend, from Rexroth to Duncan and from Hitchcock
To Lorca but anthologies such as The Rag and Bone
Shop of the Heart that Robert Bly, James Hillman and
Michael Meade put together at the end of the last century,
That quickly gone, 20th Century with the title, of course
Taken from William Butler Yeats recognition of where
We are, and have been and are going.
                                  Strange to stop
And read over pieces of work known and forgotten or even
Poems that I should have read a life ago, finding friends
And wanting to ask questions about the whys and
Wherefores while smiling at this one view or wincing
With the hurt that this other poem elicits once again.
Poets who only read their own work remind me of farmers
Who only eat the bread made of the wheat they grow.
Food for the soul comes from all around the world
And pain felt by a soldier in the Spanish Civil War
Is not different from the amputee's pain whose head
And torso are all that remain of him after his first tour
In Afghanistan.
                From the Iliad to the work of Whitman,
Dante, Neruda, Dalton, Mayakovsky, Espada, Sassoon,
Basho, Ginsberg, Byron, Blake, Rimbaud, Petrarch,
Rumi, Sharon Olds and Carolyn Forché I find words
Put together to teach me once again that Love
And Anger, Sorrow, Compassion, Teaching, Life
And Death all have their say in the writings
That are left for us as treasures to be shared
By all of those who are yet to come or those others
Fortunate enough, like me, who have come back
To be with them once again to share their words and hearts.

An Empire's End

After Constantine could anyone have foreseen
How quickly the Roman Empire would crumble
And fall into the pieces that we still can see
And admire today?
                      And before Napoleon had
Mustered his four hundred thousand Grenadiers
And all the other soldiers in his forceful armies
To head into the Russian winter that stopped him cold,
Did anyone at all foresee that rout and absolute
Disaster of Waterloo, that left only memories behind.

With all we know of the capriciousness of history
Would any one at all have dreamt that perhaps
The disaster of 9/11 had been orchestrated and
Started the plunge of our own nation into a war
Whose outcome is certain to reverberate into
The centuries to come as the beginning of another
End?
      We, alive and still relatively well,
See markets fall, and torture and genocide
Accepted as required. In this we are all complicit
And even with the best of intentions cannot
Change the pull of gravity or the inevitability
Of our own Empire's end.
                          It does seem possible that
Unless we change our ways and change ourselves
Our stories and all we've ever known could come
To be nothing more than a small disturbance
In the galactic scheme of stars and planets
In this, the Universe we call our own.

Poem For Beni Israel

Beni has impeccable taste
And incredible luck
When those two go together
He wins ~
        So many of us
Have great luck and no taste at all
Others have great taste and
No luck at all.
              This makes
For him to have the most
Beautiful women in his life
And more than satisfactory
Financial returns in the
Working life he has chosen
For himself and his family

So rare but so wonderful
When it occurs.

Another Way Of Looking At It

In the second grade the six year old girl
Asks Miss Sandoval, "What is War?"
"Where is it?" "What do they mean
"When they say they're going to War?"
"Where is that place?"
                       Miss Sandoval replies
"It's where people fight and kill each other,
"When countries argue and can't agree and where
"One country or a group wants to control another,
"They fight, they go to War."
                       "Like a whole country
"Can get drunk and angry or jealous like Paco's uncle
"Gets when he gets drunk and gets into a fight?"
The girl asked.
            "No, not like that" the teacher said
"But come to think of it, you may be right."

We Are Fortunate

We, as poets, are indeed fortunate to be
Unlike other artists, painters or musicians
Who need instruments to make their arts
Become alive; to be seen or heard, while
We, few and happy as we are, only require
Our breath, our voice, our mind and our
Imagination to project our visions and to
Have our music reach the hearts of our
Various listeners.
                With us, our bodies
Become instruments — using words,
Our voices create ships to carry listeners
Across oceans while the slap of waves and
The whistling of the winds accompany
Our audiences to lands yet undiscovered.

Our breath can easily become the sound of crowds
Or that of a suitor imploring the beloved. We
Learn to voice the words that will convince
The listener to feel and to react to the many
Things we choose.
                Taught by birds and waterfalls,
By thunder and by falling rain, we translate
Sound into our heart's refrain so as to share
Our feelings and our visions with all who
Come to listen with open hearts and smiles.

Honoring All Veterans

We who have served this country
As well as those whom we have served
Living and dead are here to recognize,
Commemorate and honor today and
For all time to come the service
Rendered, the battles fought and won.

So we are here to plant this tree
That will stand and grow and
Extend its branches into the future
With each leaf shimmering in the sun
Recalling one life at a time joyfully
Dancing in the wind and enduring
All kinds of weather as we did
When in service on battle fields
And on the sea.   Let this tree stand
And grow and let all future visitors
Know that it was planted with heart
And recognition, with honor, love
And with pride to grow into the future
For all of us.

Curious

We have had all the technology
To put a man on the moon
And establish a station
In interstellar space.

As we knew how to settle the West
We blew up Hiroshima and Nagasaki
And made a mistake in Chernobyl
And we have done it all with money.

Our money, their money and all
The money that has to be printed
To pay for Trinity and the cruisers
That navigate the seas of the world.

They have been so smart in building
The tools of destruction and have
Evidence of how successful they are.

What would it take to reverse the course
Of our intellect and ingenuity to build
Effective engines of peace instead
Of the fantastic engines of war?

What if medals of honor were to be
Designed and distributed to all
Those worthy individuals and companies
Who establish the new commission
Of peace with power.

                 It might
Even be amusing in an age of plenty
To look back and see how stupid
The swords and lances, guns and muskets
Tanks and planes and aircraft carriers
And destroyers were in the Age of Money.

VICTOR DI SUVERO was born in Italy in 1927, grew up in China and came to the United States with his family as a political refugee in early 1941. When the Second World War broke out he was too young to be accepted in the Armed Forces, so he went to sea as a Merchant Seaman when he was 16. After the war he went to the University of California at Berkeley where he received his BA in Political Science in 1949. At Berkeley he had been the editor of the *Occident,* the literary magazine of the University and won the *Ina Coolbrith Prize* for Poetry in that year.

He then went into business and established Design and Color Service in San Francisco in 1951, going on to become a Real Estate and Mortgage Broker and Developer of real estate and mining projects for the next 32 years.

His publications include: *Salt and the Heart's Horizons,* Greenwood Press 1951; *Sight Poems,* Stolen Paper Editions, 1962; *San Francisco Poems* and *The Net,* 1987; *Tesuque Poems,* 1993; *Naked Heart,* 1997; and *Harvest Time* in 2001. He edited *¡Saludos!,* the first bilingual collection of the poetry of New Mexico, all published by Pennywhistle Press which he established in 1986.

As a poetry activist he served as a Director of the National Poetry Association for four years participating in the management of the Second National Poetry Week in San Francisco in 1987. After moving to New Mexico in 1988, di Suvero became one of the founders of PEN New Mexico, the New Mexico Book Association, and the Poetry Center of New Mexico.

Di Suvero now lives in La Villita, New Mexico on a ranch on the Rio Grande, halfway between Santa Fe and Taos and continues living a life in Poetry among his other interests.

Ordering Information
Email: vdisuvero@newmexico.com

www.ingramcontent.com/pod-product-compliance
Lightning Source LLC
Chambersburg PA
CBHW070313100426
42743CB00011B/2444